The Animal in

is very plain to see

Written by **Laurie C. Tye**   Photography by **Thomas D. Mangelsen**

WestWinds Press®

When I am hungry,
I am like a great
grizzly bear
with my mouth
wide open.

When I am scared,
I am like a white-
tailed deer who is
easily spooked.

When I am angry,
    I am like a ferocious
lion protecting his pride.

When I am curious,
I am like a spotted owl
scanning the forest floor
checking things out.

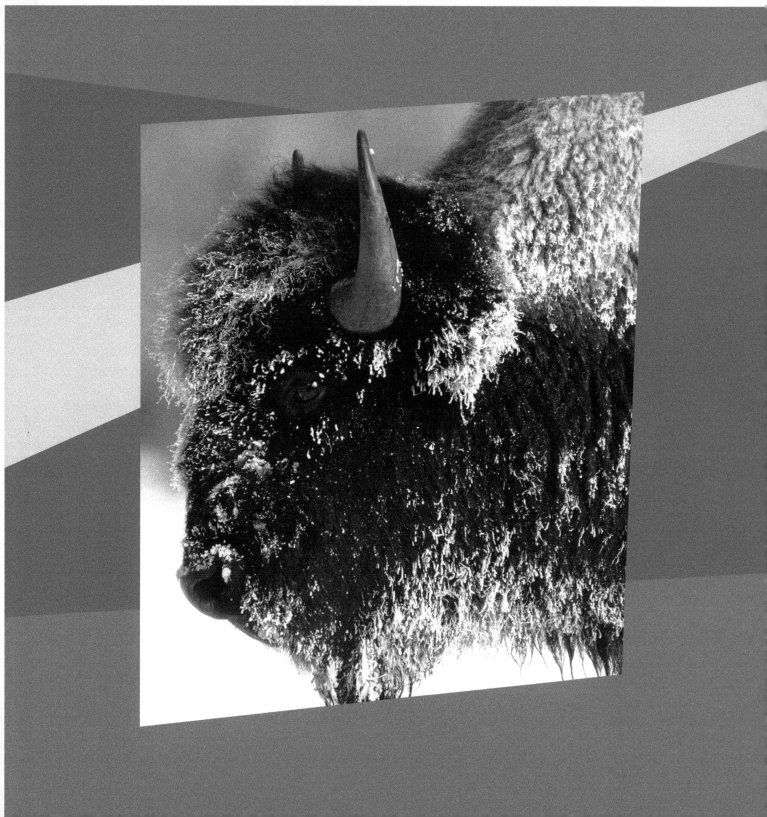

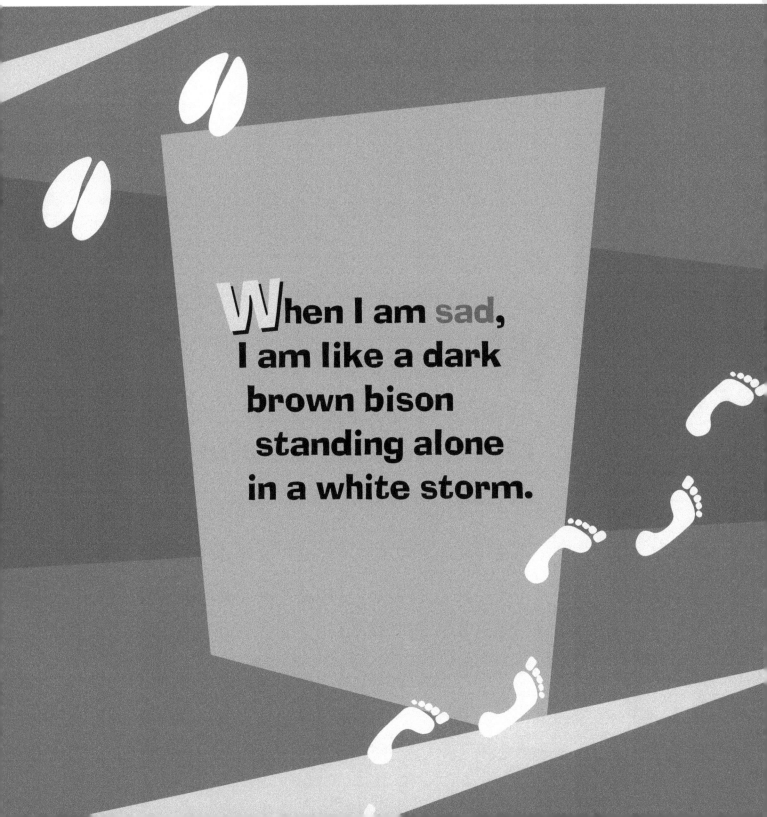

When I am sad, I am like a dark brown bison standing alone in a white storm.

When I feel like screaming, I am like a coyote howling under a full moon.

Z Z Z Z Z Z Z Z Z Z Z Z Z Z Z Z Z Z

When I am lazy, I am like a harbor seal gazing into the bright blue sky.

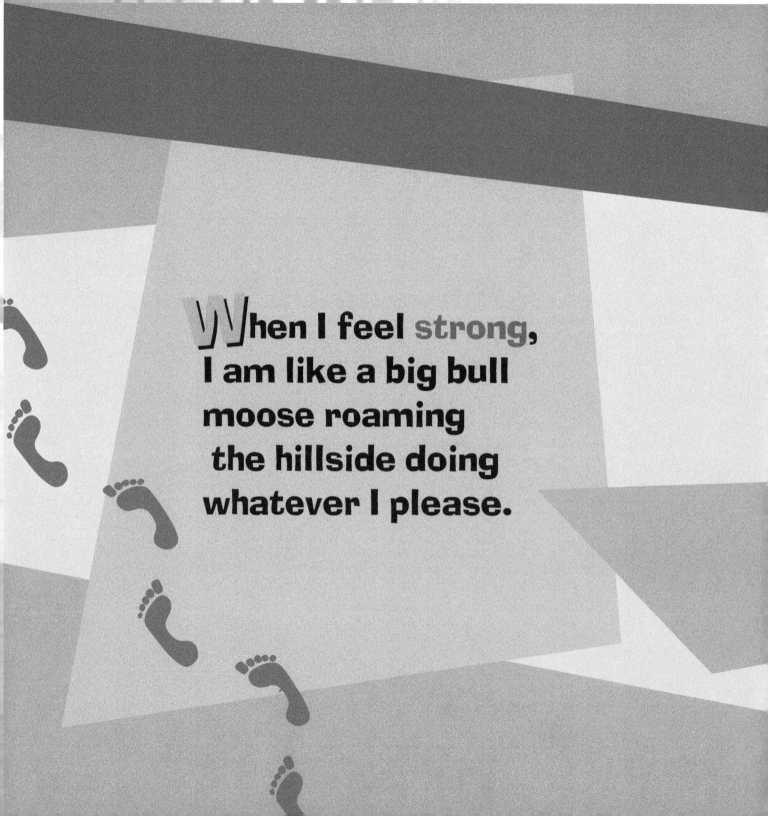

When I feel strong,
I am like a big bull
moose roaming
the hillside doing
whatever I please.

When I am excited,
I am like a little
hummingbird constantly
fluttering about.

When I am graceful, I am like a beautiful swan with my wings wide open.

When I am fast,
I am like a cheetah
chasing a gazelle.

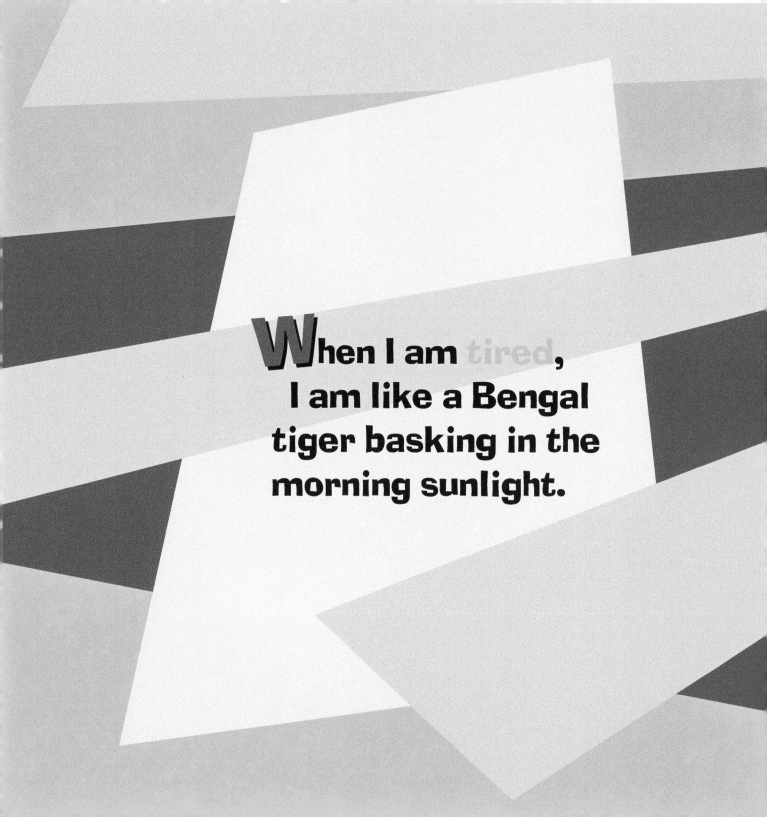

When I am tired,
I am like a Bengal
tiger basking in the
morning sunlight.

When I am having fun, I am like a polar bear playing with my best friend.

When I feel loved, I am like a mountain lion cub snuggled in my mom's arms . . .

Because she loves me more than any animal in the whole world.

Goodnight animals . . .

I am
going to
bed.

For my Aunt Helen Grennan, who has inspired
my love of animals. —T. M.

For Teea, Braden, Janessa, Lauren, and Dallen for inspiring me and
allowing me to be creative. I love you. —L. T.

Text © 2005 by Laurie Tye
Photographs © 2005 by Thomas Mangelsen

Library of Congress Cataloging-in-Publication Data

Tye, Laurie C.
  The animal in me—is very plain to see / by Laurie C. Tye ; photography by Thomas D. Mangelsen.
      p. cm.
  ISBN 1-55868-864-1 (hardbound) — ISBN 1-55868-898-6 (softbound)
  1. Emotions—Juvenile literature. 2. Animal behavior—Juvenile literature. I. Mangelsen, Thomas D.,
ill. II. Title.
  BF561.T94 2005
  152.4—dc22

                                                                    2005002674

WestWinds Press®
An imprint of Graphic Arts Center Publishing Company
P.O. Box 10306, Portland, Oregon 97296-0306
503-226-2402 • www.gacpc.com

President/Publisher: Charles M. Hopkins
Associate Publisher: Douglas A. Pfeiffer
Editorial Staff: Timothy W. Frew, Tricia Brown, Jean Andrews,
Kathy Howard, Jean Bond-Slaughter
Production Staff: Richard L. Owsiany, Susan Dupere
Design: Vicki Knapton

Printed in the United States of America